Original title:
The Oasis of Dreams

Copyright © 2025 Creative Arts Management OÜ
All rights reserved.

Author: Cassandra Whitaker
ISBN HARDBACK: 978-1-80581-560-0
ISBN PAPERBACK: 978-1-80581-087-2
ISBN EBOOK: 978-1-80581-560-0

A Sanctuary of the Heart's Yearnings

In a land where wishes wear bright hats,
And all the squirrels dance with the cats,
Bubbles float by, laughing so loud,
While dreams wear pajamas, feeling so proud.

A river flows with cherry soda,
Where raindrops play hopscotch, what a go-getter!
Flip-flops sing songs to the jellybeans,
As stars juggle planets in moonlit scenes.

Big marshmallow clouds hold secret chats,
While gumdrop flowers spread out their mats,
Ticklish shadows chase after the light,
In this carnival of dreams, oh what a sight!

So grab your hat and don't be late,
Join the parade at this magical gate,
Where laughter is the most treasured art,
Welcome, dear friend, to the dharma of heart!

Threads of Light in Gritty Tales

In a tale where shadows mix,
A cat wore socks to fix,
A pot of gold turned out to be,
Just beans with a side of brie.

The hero lost a shoe one day,
While dancing in a wild display,
He tripped on a dancing bear,
And rose up with a funny glare.

Oasis of the Forgotten Muse

A painter's brush dipped in jam,
Created skies with a loud slam,
His cows painted blue, oh what a sight,
They mooed in rhythm, what a delight!

The poet wrote with jelly beans,
In verses sweet like candy scenes,
Yet every rhyme just fell apart,
As he snacked instead of taking part.

Celestial Pools of Reflection

Upon a pool of wobbly light,
Swam a fish in a funny fight,
He wore a hat with polka dots,
And boasted of his tasty thoughts.

The frogs nearby sang silly tunes,
While juggling colorful balloons,
They leapt and slipped in such a way,
Creating laughs that filled the day.

Secrets Amidst the Shimmering Sands

In sands that whispered silly jokes,
Lived crabs that dressed as tiny folks,
With top hats made from macaroni,
They danced around like they were phony.

Beneath the sun, a treasure's grin,
Was just a rusty old trash bin,
Yet all the critters gathered 'round,
To laugh at what they all had found.

Ethereal Calm Amidst the Parched

In a desert where mirages play,
I saw a llama wearing a toupee.
He danced with flair and sang a tune,
While sipping tea beneath the moon.

The cactus cracked a silly joke,
A tumbleweed began to poke.
Their laughter echoed through the sand,
As if tickled by a magic hand.

Palette of Daydreams and Delights

Colors splashed across the sky,
Chickens in capes began to fly.
With every shade, their antics grew,
Bright hues of mischief, all askew.

Pies danced round in jubilee,
For pastry folks, such glee to see!
They tossed cream pies with giddy cheer,
While giggling clouds rolled in, so near.

Blossoms on the Edge of Reality

Roses wore the latest styles,
With sunglasses and toothy smiles.
Tulips pranced like they were stars,
Jiving to the beat of Mars.

But daisies tripped on their own feet,
Creating chaos, oh what a feat!
While daffodils played peek-a-boo,
Who knew flowers had such fun to do?

Harvest of Whimsy in the Wasteland

On fields of corn, the scarecrows groan,
Crafting poems all alone.
They write of beans and banana peels,
With high hopes for their quirky meals.

A wind-up mouse led them in song,
In this land where oddities belong.
They chuckled loud, with hearts so free,
In a realm of pure absurdity.

Rapture in the Silence

A duck in a tux, oh what a sight,
He quacks with a flair, quite a delight.
A cow brings dessert, is that cream-filled pie?
In silence we laugh, as the moments fly.

Balloons in the breeze dance a silly jig,
While a cat tries to dance, but fits like a twig.
With whispers of giggles hidden in green,
The hush of the gathering is pure comic sheen.

Mirage of Tomorrow

A llama in shades makes quite the parade,
With a dazzling grin that could never fade.
He struts through the sand like he owns the place,
While we laugh so hard, we can't keep our face.

The sun makes a splash on a biscuit so grand,
A superhero snail just zips through the sand.
Tomorrow we'll meet for a picnic in flight,
Where jellybeans rain, and all troubles feel light.

Reflections of the Heart

A mirror that talks with a wink and a smile,
Tells tales of my socks that were lost for a while.
It chuckles at blunders that I can't outsmart,
Reflecting my quirks, oh, a true work of art.

With giggles and snorts, the laughter unfolds,
At how my best plans turn to popcorn and mold.
We dance with the shadows and giggle with glee,
In the joyous echo of what's silly in me.

Serendipity's Edge

A penguin in flip-flops, now that's a true look,
He waddles with style, writes poems in a book.
With fish in the air, and jokes on the floor,
We sip at our soda, and eagerly roar.

The moon wears a hat, as it winks at the sun,
While we twirl to the beat, oh, this night's just begun.
At the edge of our whims, we laugh and we play,
In a world where the funny just brightens the day.

Currents of Enchantment

In a land where socks come alive,
They dance and twirl; they strive.
With mismatched shoes, they chase a hare,
While giggles float upon the air.

Here carpets fly with absurd ease,
As ducks discuss the shape of cheese.
A river flows with fizzy drinks,
And wise old trees throw winks and blinks.

Gnomes play chess with fainting moons,
While dancing spoons hum merry tunes.
A pickle here, a jelly there,
Each step's a joke, a silly care.

So dip your toes in whimsy's stream,
Where every thought's a playful dream.
What sights await just round the bend?
In this mad world, there's no end!

Moonlit Refuge

Beneath the glow of cheese-shaped moon,
Clowns juggle stars; it's quite the boon.
With lollipop trees and rainbow streams,
We laugh at life's most silly schemes.

Chickens wear hats and bake a pie,
While raccoons plot a starry sky.
Whispers of laughter, wide-eyed pets,
A feast of fun, no regrets yet.

A moonbeam trampoline's the place,
Where dreams do somersaults with grace.
Balloons with faces float and cheer,
Each giggle heard is music clear.

So dance on clouds of cotton candy,
Where nothing ever feels too dandy.
In this bright nook, we let hearts roam,
Finding pure joy, we call it home!

Treasures of the Mindscape

In the chest of thoughts, a treasure glows,
With tiny critters in colorful clothes.
Each idea bounces like a spring,
In this wacky realm, absurd is king.

There's a penguin painting on the wall,
With lemon zest that has no gall.
Silly secrets in every nook,
Discover gems in a storybook.

Marshmallow clouds, they giggle and shift,
As dreams play hide and seek, a drift.
A maze of laughs that twists and bends,
Where every bend brings playful friends.

So stock your mind with heaps of cheer,
Let laughter echo far and near.
In this wild space where thoughts unwind,
You'll find the treasures of the mind.

Garden of Respite

In a garden where the daisies sing,
Bees wear crowns while butterflies swing.
With silly plants that tickle your toes,
Laughter blossoms wherever it goes.

Gnomes sip tea from acorn cups,
While rabbits jump through syruped ups.
Sunflowers grin with goofy leans,
In this patch, joy bursts at the seams.

A lazy cat, in shades and flair,
Chases balloons that float in air.
With every bloom, a jest is sprouted,
In laughter's arms, none are doubt abouted.

So wander here, and shed your woes,
With giggles wrapped in pollen's prose.
Planting smiles in the soil's embrace,
In this merry patch, find your place!

Wandering Spirits

In a land where the camels do dance,
The sand tickles toes in a funny romance.
The spirits are lost with a giggling cheer,
Chasing mirages that vanish from here.

A parrot's wisecrack makes everyone laugh,
As shadows play cards and split a tall half.
With the stars as our guides, we twirl and we sway,
In a world where the sand is our stage for play.

Horizons of Hopes

Under a sky painted bright with a smile,
Dreams hop on clouds and dance for a while.
Each blow of the wind is a chuckle rare,
As hopes sail on ships made of candy and air.

Darts of sunshine tickle, make us all grin,
While the waves tell tales of the friends we've been.
Here, time wears a hat that's too big for its head,
And laughter is the feast that we all love to spread.

Whispered Secrets of Solitude

In the quiet of night, where shadows do creep,
Thoughts play hopscotch while the world's fast asleep.
Voices of whispers tickle dreams like a tease,
With secrets that giggle like leaves in the breeze.

A cat with a monocle gazes with pride,
While giggling at riddles that wander outside.
In solitude wrapped in a blanket of fun,
The moon plays the jester until night is done.

Tides of Tranquility

The waves have come dressed in bright polka dots,
Cannonball splashes, oh what funny spots!
They whisper hush-hush, as they wiggle and sway,
In their watery dance, they giggle away.

Seagulls join in with a clumsy ballet,
Squawking their jokes in a loud, funny way.
As sea foam erupts with a shimmering cheer,
We roll with the tides, feeling no hint of fear.

A Place for Wishes to Wander

In a land where socks gain fame,
And unicorns play chess all day,
You'll find a tree with candy leaves,
That whispers secrets on its sway.

The clouds wear hats of vibrant hue,
While jellybeans bounce on the grass,
Here every wish is polka-dotted,
And dreams all gather for a laugh.

Watch the fish that dance on land,
With roller skates, they glide with glee,
They sing of cookies, warm and sweet,
While twirling 'round a sugar tree.

So come and leave your cares behind,
Let silly joy take hold of you,
In this silly world of wacky fun,
Where wishes fly like kangaroos.

Ethereal Refuge of the Soul

In a field where daisies giggle loud,
And tea parties host few grumpy gnomes,
The sun brings pies instead of rays,
As laughter loops like happy poems.

A frog in glasses reads the news,
While sipping soup from a giant shoe,
The wind hums tunes of silly dreams,
As squirrels debate which dance to do.

Clouds are fluffy marshmallow dreams,
Hiding secrets, oh so sly,
They tickle noses as they float,
While sunbeams wink and say, 'Oh my!'

So come restore your weary heart,
In this silly realm where hopes take flight,
You'll find a friend in every tree,
And joy will be your guiding light.

Serenity Beneath the Starlit Sky

Beneath the twinkling starry winks,
Where marshmallows rain from the night,
A moonbeam rides a bicycle,
As comets join a disco fight.

Grass blades whisper jokes to trees,
As owls become the DJ crew,
The crickets chirp a funky beat,
And fireflies flash a light show too.

A picnic blanket made of dreams,
Serves sandwiches of pure delight,
With soda that sings a happy tune,
While cupcakes hold a dance-off right.

So lay your head on pillows soft,
And let the silliness unwind,
In this playful, starry wonder,
Where every giggle is aligned.

Ciphers in the Grain of Time

Time scribbles notes in the sand,
As clocks wear hats and chuckle loud,
The past and future play hopscotch,
While giggling with the dreamy crowd.

Beans hold meetings, full of schemes,
As squirrels plot a nutty heist,
The walls of Time are made of cake,
And laughter is the best of spice.

Each tick-tock plays a goofy tune,
A jester hops from year to year,
In every grain, a joke awaits,
For laughter is the treasure here.

So come decode these playful lines,
And dance through moments, light as air,
In this whimsical world of joy,
Where every heartbeat has a flair.

Cradle of Fantasies Unfurled

In a land where cacti wear hats,
And camels dance in silly spats,
Sand dunes whisper jokes from afar,
While lizards strum on an old guitar.

A mirage of ice cream appears,
With sprinkles made of sunny cheers,
Palm trees sway to a jazzy beat,
As monkeys serve us fruity treats.

Beneath a sky of candy hue,
We dodge the flying rubber shoe,
Giggling at the playful chase,
In this bizarre and joyous place.

When night falls, the stars all wear socks,
And glow-in-the-dark laughing rocks,
With dreams that tickle all around,
In this silly, fantasy ground.

The Desert's Heartbeat of Yearning

There's a cactus trying to flirt,
With a curious camel in a skirt,
They plan a date by the moonlight,
To dance and laugh through the night.

Sandcastles built with a twist,
Every grain has a terrible twist,
The king is a surfing sand crab,
Living life without a small blab.

The sun's a big orange cream puff,
Its rays giving goofy stuff,
While tumbleweeds play peek-a-boo,
Silly antics—they make quite the crew.

Under stars that giggle and wink,
We ponder what we dare to drink,
Sipping on dreams from a bucket near,
In this land full of funny cheer.

Mirage of Forgotten Tomorrows

Once I saw a goat wearing shoes,
Trotting down with oddball news,
It bleated tales of lost socks,
Helping travelers find their blocks.

Pigs fly high with a splash and a twirl,
While desert owls dance and twirl,
A date palm juggles watermelons,
Splashing laughter in our felons.

The horizon shouts with playful glee,
Chasing shadows and sipping tea,
Sandstorms laugh, wearing clown wigs,
As we glide by on magic squigs.

In the quiet, a turtle does tap,
Leading us to a funny map,
Where every step is a joyous shout,
Of forgotten dreams we can't live without.

Embrace of the Endless Horizon

On the edge of a glowing day,
Silly whispers blow us away,
Birds wear hats and sing off key,
While bees collaborate in harmony.

The sun and moon play hopscotch rounds,
Creating laughter with their sounds,
A grand parade of wandering dreams,
Where hilarity bursts at the seams.

Pineapple cacti belt out tunes,
Beneath the laughing silver moons,
Fish in sandals splash along,
In a world where nothing is wrong.

With every chuckle, we leap and bound,
In this land where smiles surround,
Together we dance, we twirl and hum,
In the embrace of funny, we become.

Whispers of Tranquil Sands

In a land where camels trot,
I found a snack, but it was not.
A mirage of a cheeseburger,
I caught a glimpse, though it did not linger.

Sand castles built with care,
But a wind blew, oh, such despair!
They fell apart like a bad joke,
Laughter erupted—oh, what a poke!

Belly flops in waters warm,
Splashing friends, we cause a storm.
But with each splash, a funny fail,
We laugh until we turn pale.

The sun dips low, a playful tease,
Chasing shadows with such ease.
In this land, we dance and wiggle,
Life here is a joyful giggle.

Mirage of Hope

A fountain sprouted in my head,
But it turned out a garden shed.
With plants that danced and laughed at me,
Flowers wore hats, so silly, see?

I followed paths of golden sand,
Hoping for treasures not so bland.
But found a shoe, a single flip,
Next to it, my sandwich took a trip!

The cacti waved with arms so wide,
As I attempted a graceful slide.
I tripped and fell, what a delight,
I looked up, and they were just polite!

Stars above, they wink and twinkle,
The moon joins in with a friendly crinkle.
In this land of upside down,
Laughter reigns—the crown's my frown!

Sanctuary of Slumber

As I lay on soft, warm sand,
I dreamed of pizza, oh so grand.
But the crust was made of fluffy clouds,
And fairies cheered in joyful crowds.

A snore escaped, the turtles laughed,
As I napped, thinking of my draft.
They stole my hat, those sneaky beasts,
While I snoozed, they threw a feast!

When I woke, a parade passed by,
Led by lizards, oh my, oh my!
They danced in shoes made of grass,
Twirled around, oh what a class!

A lullaby sung by the breeze,
With whispers that tickled my knees.
In this spot where smiles bloom,
I chuckled softly, dispelling gloom.

Celestial Mirage

Stars above shine like bright pies,
A celestial feast before our eyes.
We tried to catch one for a snack,
But they giggled and flitted back!

The moon fashioned a giant scoop,
As we attempted a wacky loop.
With laughter echoing through the night,
The desert joined our frolic light!

In this place where shadows play,
And tumbleweeds roll along the way.
We danced till dawn, our hearts so free,
With mirages of joy as far as we could see.

As daylight broke with silly pranks,
We drew in sand with interlaced ranks.
With each giggle, the world seemed bright,
In our quirky kingdom, oh, what a sight!

Ribbons of Illusion

In a land where socks fly free,
And etiquette's a mystery,
A cat wears shades, oh what a sight,
While dancing frogs embrace the night.

Teacups chatter, gossip flows,
A rooster struts in fancy clothes,
The sun wears a grin, so bold and wide,
As butterflies take a thrilling slide.

Clouds become marshmallows sweet,
Where laughter and wild rhythms meet,
The moon throws confetti from up high,
Each pixelated star begins to fly.

Here nonsense reigns and quirks collide,
A pinball wizard takes us for a ride,
In this curious world, we all belong,
As we dance the night away, sing our song.

Heart's Safe Haven

In cozy corners, giggles bloom,
With cookie crumbs that spell out 'zoom',
The painting smiles, can you believe?
It winked at me, oh what a tease!

Kittens roll in yarns divine,
While penguins try to do the line,
Each tickle of laughter lights the air,
Silly moments will take us anywhere.

Waffles wear hats, a grand parade,
With syrup rivers that never fade,
The sun dodges clouds, they play hide and seek,
In this warm space, all the absurd seems chic.

We bounce with joy on dreary days,
Finding magic in quirky ways,
Each heartbeat whispers secret schemes,
In our silly retreat, we chase our dreams.

Sunlit Dreams

Where bubbles float and goats wear ties,
Each shadow dances, oh what a surprise,
The sun's a jester in a golden hat,
While strawberries chat with a friendly cat.

Lemonade rivers flow with glee,
As candy fish swim wild and free,
A squirrel laughs, juggling acorns bright,
In this whimsical world, all feels right.

Dancers in pajamas prance around,
While playful echoes play their sound,
Tickling tunes from the trees above,
In this sunlit place, we find our love.

With dreams that bounce on cotton clouds,
We'll paint our faces in bright pink shrouds,
As ice cream cones melt without a care,
In laughter's embrace, we're floating in air.

Waters that Whisper

By bubbling brooks, the fish wear specs,
As frogs sing ballads about their checks,
The reeds gossip in a sassy sway,
In this funny kingdom, we splash and play.

The moon dives in for a chilly swim,
While ducks discuss the latest whim,
Every ripple tells a silly tale,
As laughing waves begin to sail.

Rainboots strut along the sandy shore,
Each splash brings forth a roaring score,
A sea of giggles is what we crave,
In the joyous current, we feel so brave.

With buckets full of dreams afloat,
We ride the tide on a rubber boat,
In the waters of whimsy, lives a cheer,
As the gushing laughter draws us near.

Haven of Serenity

In a place where cactus dance,
Even lizards take a chance,
They wear hats and shades, it's true,
Sipping juice beneath the blue.

Palm trees gossip, sway and twirl,
While sand dunes form a charming swirl,
A picnic with the wildest crew,
Camels play cards, if you only knew!

Laughter floats on breezy nights,
Glowworms twinkle, shining lights,
In this spot where dreams take flight,
A mirage of a cake in sight!

So if you need a quirky space,
Join the fun in this wild place,
Where silly thoughts and giggles blend,
And the jokes are never at an end.

Dreams by the Water's Edge

By the edge where ripples play,
Fish sing songs in their own way,
They wear tuxedos, quite absurd,
With bubbles dancing, barely heard.

The ducks in bowties take a stroll,
Over water, they float and roll,
With splashes loud, they make a scene,
Chasing each other—feathered and green.

Bubbles rise like tiny dreams,
Laughing at the sunlight beams,
In this splashy, goofy show,
Nothing serious, just go with the flow.

So bring your quirks and silly hats,
Join in with all the feathered chats,
At the edge where laughter's sound,
Makes every heart a little round.

Echoes of the Desert

In the desert, echoes giggle,
Cacti snicker, bushes wiggle,
Sand that tickles, winds that dance,
A silly world where dreams prance.

The sun slips down with a wink,
As tumbleweeds begin to think,
Of all the pranks they want to pull,
Rolling on, they feel quite full.

Lizards flaunt their vibrant skin,
Creating swagger, wearing a grin,
They host a party in the sand,
Where humor reigns, oh isn't it grand?

So come and join this silly quest,
In the land where laughter's blessed,
Where echoes sound like playful shouts,
And joy is what this place is about.

Beneath the Crescent Moon

Beneath a smile of silver light,
Critters gather, what a sight,
Dancing shadows, laughter rings,
Chasing dreams, oh what fun things!

A raccoon in a tiny coat,
Twirls around, how he can float,
While owls hoot like old wise fools,
Dancing under starry jewels.

The night air filled with teasing jest,
As laughter puts all worries to rest,
In this bright, whimsical space,
Even nightingales want to race!

So come and laugh amid the stars,
Forget your troubles, heal your scars,
For under this enchanting moon,
Life's a funny, joyful tune.

Gentle Ripples of Reverie

In the desert of my mind, I roam,
Searching for a cozy home.
Sandwiches fly with mustard wings,
Laughter's tune, oh how it sings!

Cacti wear hats of pink and blue,
They tease the sun, and it giggles too.
A mirage dances, waves hello,
Join the fun, come see the show!

Camels tell jokes with a sly cheek,
While tumbleweeds play hide and seek.
Stars wink down, playing prankster's part,
As dreams take flight, a funny art!

In this whimsical wanderland,
Dreams bounce like a rubber band.
With giggles echoing through the night,
Join the laughter, it feels so right!

Cascades of Calm

A waterfall of giggles flows,
As rubber ducks wear fancy clothes.
In this stream of thought and glee,
Fish wear glasses, can't you see?

The rocks are singing silly tunes,
While crickets dance with silver spoons.
Bubbles pop with jokes profound,
As laughter ripples all around.

Turtles drag race while they quack,
A chill-out zone on memory's track.
Waves of humor crash ashore,
Who knew life's a comedy chore?

Through tranquil paths, we take a ride,
Where silliness dances, dreams collide.
In this calm, we find delight,
With chuckles echoing through the night!

Where Dreams Flow

In the river of my fancies bright,
Socks float by, in colors of light.
They giggle and splash with a happy cheer,
Waving at ducks that paddle near.

The shadows play hopscotch on the sand,
While ants form a marching band.
Mice in tuxedos tap dance away,
On the banks where dreamers play.

Clouds send whispers on gentle beams,
Tickling wishes, igniting dreams.
Bubblegum trees sway to the beat,
As joy-filled hearts skip a sweet treat!

In this realm where laughter flows,
Tickle the echoes, let joy expose.
With glee and whimsy, let's take a chance,
In this quirky, funny dream dance!

Threads of Peace

Woven threads of laughter bright,
Spin a tapestry of delight.
The loom's a place where giggles meet,
With friendships tied, life's bittersweet.

Knitted clouds, spun from pure bliss,
Whispering secrets of a silly kiss.
Puppies in pajamas jump and twirl,
Making the whole wide world unfurl.

Yarn balls bounce, eager to play,
Stitching together a joyous day.
Dreams are buttons on this thread,
Each a story waiting to spread.

In a patchwork quilt of cheer and fun,
We find our peace, life just begun.
Sewn with love, laughter, and play,
In every stitch, we find our way!

The Dance of Light and Shadow

In a world where sunlight beams,
The shadows waltz with fervent dreams.
They twist and twirl, a quirky pair,
A game of hopscotch in the air.

The sun makes faces, grins so wide,
While shadows giggle, can't abide.
They play peek-a-boo behind the trees,
As if the wind's a tease with ease.

A chicken clucks, the sun starts to pout,
While shadows dance, they twist about.
Their merry jig on hot pavement heats,
They dodge the feet, with nimble beats.

The moon will join, a crescent smile,
With stars that wink, if just a while.
Together they'll chuckle, sing their tune,
As twilight whispers, "See you soon!"

Tales from the Quiet Pool

A twig that floats upon the smile,
The water ripples, plays the while.
Frogs tell jokes, with goofy grins,
While fishes laugh at all our sins.

Some ducks quack tales of silly fright,
Of late-night snacks and woeful bites.
A wave, a splash, a comedic fall,
They gather 'round, the best of all.

A turtle cheers, "I'll win this race,"
But all he does is change his pace.
A crab cracks jokes, oh so refined,
While minnows swim with comical minds.

So if you're lost, don't swim away,
Join the fun with pond's array.
Hear the giggles, don't be a fool,
Behind each splash, a goofy duel!

Embrace of the Stillness

In the quiet nook where silence hums,
The wind plays tunes, a funny drum.
A squirrel sneezes, branches shake,
While crickets laugh, no time to fake.

The leaves nod gently, comic relief,
As shadows draw their well-timed grief.
A cat sprawls out, a jester bold,
In this calm jest where stories unfold.

Boring moments? Oh, not a chance,
With nature hosting its lively dance.
A beetle rolls with wobbly glee,
Sliding on leaves, capering free.

So wrap up tight in this still cocoon,
Where laughter lingers like an old tune.
Embrace the calm, it's quite a jest,
In stillness, we're truly at our best.

Safe Harbor of Thoughts

An anchor drops in a sea of jest,
With boats that bob and love to quest.
Ideas tumble like sailor's hats,
As laughter echoes, "What of that?"

Dolphins dive to join the fair,
With squeaks and chirps, oh what a pair!
The waves, they whisper, "Join the fun,"
While seagulls squawk 'til day is done.

A treasure map made of silly riddles,
Points to pirate jokes, swashbuckling twiddles.
The compass spins, a merry whirl,
As thoughts collide, a playful twirl.

In this safe harbor, minds set sail,
With nets of giggles and laughter's hail.
So chart your course, be not aloof,
In this sea, you're the captain—sweet proof!

Glistening Waters of Longing

In a pool that sparkles bright,
The ducks wear hats, what a sight!
Swim with thoughts, don't take a dive,
Where dreams float by, oh how they thrive.

A fish with shades swims by with flair,
It offers jokes, if you can bear.
Laughter bubbles, splashes loud,
In this place, we feel so proud.

Coconut drinks with tiny straws,
Mermaids gossip without a pause.
They giggle and sway, what a show,
Here with my friends, the fun won't slow.

And when the sun begins to set,
We dance, forget what we regret.
This silly spot where dreams ignite,
A joyful twist to a starry night.

The Hidden Retreat of Aspirations

In a glen where wishes bloom,
Hats grow legs and start to zoom!
They take off, part of the crew,
Waving goodbye, 'Hey, how do you do?'

With unicorns baking pies on trees,
The squirrels laugh at their clumsy knees.
Each slice bursts with flavors divine,
Made by dreams, oh, they're so fine!

Clouds dressed as pillows float on past,
They whisper secrets, tons, and vast.
A tiny sprite plays games with fate,
In her quest to find a mate.

And while we sip our lemonade,
We watch the fun that blushes and fades.
In this hidden nook, full of cheer,
We craft our dreams without any fear.

Dreamscapes Carved in Sand

Beneath the sun, the sand does dance,
A castle rises with a chance.
The walls are made of candy floss,
Come sip with me from jelly's boss!

Seagulls squawk, their humor grand,
They try to steal our beachy sand.
But every time they make a dash,
We toss them crumbs and watch them crash.

Footprints vanish, what a joke,
The tide comes in, and soaks my cloak.
Driftwood tells the stories late,
Of mermaids dancing, oh, what a fate!

So build your dreams in grains so fine,
Where laughter dances with the brine.
As night rolls in, we'll laugh and say,
Tomorrow's sun will bring new play!

Celestial Reflections of the Mind

In a sky of blue with stars that snort,
Galaxies spin, a cosmic sport.
They tickle clouds, what a wild race,
While wishes whirl in endless space.

Each twinkling light has tales to share,
About the dreams that float in air.
They ponder life, and giggles thrive,
In this wild ride, we feel alive.

A moonbeam slips on stardust slick,
Where comets zoom and planets kick.
And laughter bursts like shooting stars,
A universe rich with giggling bars!

So grab your dreams, they're in the sky,
With every chuckle, let them fly.
In this grand show, let's share a grin,
For with each joke, we surely win!

Enigmas of the Quiet Shore

Seagulls gossip, sharing tales,
While crabs dance in their tiny scales.
A fish in shades of polka dots,
Swims wearing boots, it ties the knots.

Sandcastles rise, a monarch's claim,
With jellybeans, it's all a game.
An octopus in funky slides,
Serving coffee, where laughter abides.

Waves tickle feet of those who roam,
Jokes whispered through the frothy foam.
A starfish cracks its silly grin,
As mermaids giggle, "Where to begin?"

In this place where mirth remains,
Every shell sings silly refrains.
The tide rolls in, with tidal glee,
In sandy laughter, we're all carefree.

Journey to Tranquil Realms

A turtle wears a sunhat bright,
While humming tunes that feel just right.
Traveling slowly, what a sight,
With ladybugs that dance in flight.

Clouds puff up like marshmallow fluff,
As squirrels talk a bit too tough.
They barter nuts for outfits grand,
And giggle as they plan their stand.

Rivers chuckle, twisting wide,
As frogs in jackets leap and slide.
"Hey, wait for me!" a snail shouts out,
But in his haste, falls with a pout.

The journey sparkles, weaving jest,
In tranquil realms, we feel our best.
With laughter floating on the breeze,
Every moment, fun and easy.

Landscapes of the Soul

A garden blooms with socks and shoes,
Where every flower loves to snooze.
A butterfly in plaid does sway,
As bumblebees have something to say.

Clouds roll in, all fluffy and round,
Painting smiles on the ground.
A gopher guards his stash of jokes,
While raccoons share their daily pokes.

Colors clash like dancers at play,
In landscapes bright and wacky display.
Happiness springs from every patch,
As nature's laughter finds a match.

So come explore these jolly sights,
With giggles echoing through the nights.
In landscapes where the heart takes toll,
You'll find the corners of your soul.

Canvas of Illusions

On a canvas where the colors blend,
A cat in shades of rainbow bends.
He eats spaghetti with a fork,
And draws the stars that dance and cork.

Paintbrush penguins, waddling by,
With easels under a purple sky.
They swirl their tales with splashing hues,
While laughing at their artist blues.

A monkey swings on lines of zest,
Creating all the nonsense best.
With each stroke comes a whimsical tune,
And laughter floats like a busy loon.

So let your mind run wild and free,
In this canvas, funny as can be.
With each illusion, join the spree,
A world where dreams will always be.

Embracing Stillness

In a quiet corner, I rest and peek,
Where time takes a nap, and the sun plays hide and seek.
A cactus waves hello with arms so wide,
As I sip cactus juice, feeling quite dignified.

Lizards wear sunglasses, strutting with flair,
While tumbleweeds tango, without a care.
A jackrabbit joins in, twirling about,
With a dance so funky, I can't help but shout!

The silence is golden, but the laughter is bright,
In this whimsical space where nothing feels tight.
A mirage of giggles floats up in the air,
In the land of giggles, joy's everywhere!

So here's to the stillness, to the glee that we find,
In every small moment, we're both silly and kind.
Let's toast to the peace that tickles our soul,
In this haven of fun, we are perfectly whole.

Peering into the Mirage

I squint through the shimmer, a sight to behold,
A mirage of ice cream in this desert so bold.
With sprinkles and cherries stacked ever so high,
But it's just melting sand; oh, how time flies by!

Little critters giggle at my longing gaze,
As they roast marshmallows in the sun's wild blaze.
A dancing mirage of my sweetest retreat,
Turns out to be just a tricky sand pit!

Yet laughter erupts as I tumble and fall,
Right into a puddle, what a splashing ball!
I'm the queen of the mirage, quite soaked yet fine,
With stories to share, like desert sunshine!

So peer in the distance, let dreams float and sway,
For what's out of reach may turn giggles our way.
Just remember, dear friend, as you dream and you wish,
Mirages can evoke the silliest dish!

Dreams Beneath Starlight

Underneath the twinkle, the stars loudly hum,
While camels hold karaoke, singing to some.
The moon takes the stage, with a spotlight so bright,
As we dance in the stardust—what a whimsical night!

The wise old owl plays the tambourine slow,
While lizards breakdance, putting on quite the show.
Dreams flutter like fireflies, dancing around,
In this shimmering party, pure joy can be found!

The cacti are grooving, all prickles and glee,
While the dunes turn to pillows, oh so comfy and free.
I dip into dreams, of a jelly bean feast,
As wishes come true, from the greatest to least!

A night filled with laughter, with friends all around,
We share silly stories and giggles abound.
Under stars that shimmer, and laughter that beams,
We savor the magic of our wildest dreams!

Breaths of the Desert Night

When the sun takes a bow and the cool breezes sigh,
The night comes alive with a spark in the sky.
The critters conspire in shadows so sleek,
Planning a party—it's mischief we seek!

There's a dingo with slippers, prancing in sync,
While a lizard makes smoothies from cactus and drink.
With starlight as jazz, and the moon guiding beats,
We tap dance on sand with our very own feet!

The silence now giggles, and whispers amazed,
As we whirl 'round the campfire, joyfully crazed.
A rustle of laughter, a shimmer of light,
Breaths of the night are pure fun and delight!

So let's cozy up, in this soft, sandy bed,
With dreams that resound in the stars overhead.
The desert holds secrets, so silly and bright,
In a world painted vibrant by the beauty of night!

Ethereal Springs

In a land where the glow bugs dance,
Giggling trees wear a leafy pants,
The puddles chuckle, jump around,
Where lost socks often can be found.

The sun throws rays like a silly hat,
While cool breezes play with the chubby cat,
There's lemonade flowing from a fountain wide,
And candy clouds float on a giggly tide.

Dancing llamas whisper silly jokes,
While rainbow fish tease the clumsy folks,
A squirrel with shades rides a rollercoaster,
In this place, ordinary is a grand poster!

So grab your dreams, let's take a dive,
Where laughter and joy are always alive,
In a world where everything's a jest,
Come sip the fun, and let's be blessed!

Spheres of Serenity

Under moons where the marshmallows grow,
Balloons hold secrets, and giggles flow,
Pineapples wear hats made of dough,
While rabbits in tutus steal the show.

Stars play hopscotch on cotton candy
As jellybeans sound so dandy,
The breeze hums a tune, oh so silly,
Through giggling hills that dance like willy-nilly.

There's a sign that says 'No Serious Faces'
While turtles do waltzes in silly paces,
Cucumbers sing in the vivid sun,
And even the cupcakes want to run!

So come search for your laughter's gold,
Amidst bubbly waters, never too cold,
In this marvel of mirth, all come and see,
With joy's tickles wrapped in sweet glee!

Enchanted Waters

Waves giggle as they splash on the shore,
While seagulls dive for candy galore,
Fish wear sunglasses, sunbathing too,
While shells tell tales that are quite askew.

In the deep, where the bubbles play hide,
Mermaids sport fins of glitter and pride,
With silly seaweed tickling their toes,
They dance with the ships and fancy shows.

The piña coladas flow like a breeze,
As crabs hold conga lines under the trees,
A dolphin juggles while wearing a tie,
And each splash is a wink in the sky.

So dip your toes, let the fun begin,
In wondrous waters, let laughter spin,
For in every ripple, a chuckle awaits,
As joy sparkles in all the small states!

Ethereal Repose

In a hammock made of candy canes,
Snoozing squirrels sing cheerful refrains,
The sun wears pajamas, oh so bright,
In a slumber party that lasts all night.

Dreams float by on fluffy white beds,
Counting silly sheep with jellybean heads,
Feathered friends in tuxedos cheer,
As giggles escape from the snoozing deer.

Clouds in baseball caps throw soft pitches,
While dandelions play, dodging the glitches,
Pillows hold secrets of nightly pranks,
Whispers of joy fill the laughter banks.

So snuggle tight in this twinkling space,
Where every tickle's a smiling embrace,
For dreams sprinkled with humor will bloom,
In this restful haven, bursting with room!

Rippled Reflections

In a pond of quirky frogs,
They croak their croons and jiggy jags.
A scene so strange, you'll laugh aloud,
As they throw parties, oh so proud.

The ducks wear shades, quite the display,
Dancing around, they wiggle away.
Turtles join in, their shells do spin,
In this wild place, who'll take the win?

Fish in tuxedos, swimming so fine,
Splashed with confetti, what a divine!
They pop their fins like party balloons,
Chasing their dreams under the moon.

Rippling giggles dance on the shore,
Every splash tells tales and lore.
In this joyful whirlpool of fun,
Where laughter ripples, we're never done.

Oasis of the Mind

In a garden where thoughts sprout wild,
Ideas bounce like a playful child.
Silly notions hide 'neath the trees,
Tickling brains like a gentle breeze.

Pens are sprouting, giggles abound,
Chasing the clouds that dance around.
With a wink and a nudge, oh what a sight,
This whimsical journey, full of delight.

Cacti wearing hats, all in a row,
Crack silly jokes, putting on a show.
Sunflowers sway to a comic beat,
In this amusing retreat, oh so sweet.

So dive headfirst, don't be shy,
In this mirthful realm, let dreams fly high.
Where laughter grows on every vine,
In this mind's escape, all's truly fine.

Stardust Retreat

Fluffy clouds of cream and pie,
Floating blissfully in the sky.
Stars wear sneakers, ready to race,
Tripping on comets, what a pace!

Galaxies laugh, it's a silly tune,
Jellybean rockets zoom past the moon.
While those planets, round and chubby,
Wobble and giggle, feeling all stubby.

Shooting stars queue for a snack break,
Chomping on space cakes, make no mistake.
They throw sprinkles at each other's tails,
In this cosmic realm where humor prevails.

So pack your dreams in a comet's tail,
Join this party on a shooting trail.
In a twinkling retreat, dreams take flight,
Under laughter's embrace, pure delight.

Solitude's Embrace

In a quiet nook where shadows dance,
A cactus wears a polka-dot pants.
The whispers of wind tell jokes so sly,
Making clouds chuckle as they float by.

A pebble's laughing at a lost shoe,
While tumbleweeds are dancing two by two.
Kangaroos in shades hop down the lane,
Juggling sunshine, avoiding the rain.

Rabbits tiptoe in bright red hats,
Holding a feast for their chubby cats.
In this solo space where silliness reigns,
Bubbles of laughter ease away pains.

So sit a while in this cozy retreat,
Where solitude wraps you, oh so sweet.
In the silence, joy finds its place,
As the world fills up with a funny embrace.

Serenity's Mirage

Under the sun, my thoughts take flight,
A hamster in a wheel, racing with delight.
I toss my hat, it flies like a kite,
While squirrels laugh, it's a comical sight.

Beneath palm trees, I sip on my drink,
Forgotten my worries, don't even think.
A swimming pool made of chocolate sink,
I take a plunge, then slowly sink.

In a land where penguins wear shades,
And lemonade flows in cheerful cascades,
I dance with llamas in funny parades,
As laughter echoes, the joy never fades.

So here I bask, with sand in my toes,
Mysteries whispered by a ticklish nose.
A world where absurdity endlessly flows,
In this silly haven, who really knows?

Fragments of Elysium

In a field of donuts, I twirl with glee,
Chasing marshmallows under a giant tree.
The rainbow birds hum a symphony,
Even the ants seem to dance, oh so free.

With ping-pong tables made of sweet pie,
And clouds that bounce like balloons in the sky.
I challenge the gophers to a high-fly,
While giggles erupt, and time slips by.

Sunbathing turtles discussing their dreams,
As jellybeans burst with sparkly gleams.
Life's a joke, or so it seems,
In this patch of joy, all laughter beams.

So let's ride flamingoes in this warm glow,
In silly shoes, we glide to and fro.
With a wink and a nod, let's put on a show,
In this merry land where giggles grow.

Twilight Reflections

Under the stars, a potato sings,
Dressed as a king, oh the joy it brings.
A cactus competes in hula hoop rings,
While the moonlight dances, and laughter clings.

A disco ball spins on a makeshift boat,
While chickens attempt to learn how to float.
In twilight's glow, a playful quote:
'Why did the tomato become a devotee of hope?'

Clouds puff cotton candy in a row,
As jellyfish tango in a radiant show.
Kangaroos bouncing, stealing the show,
In this strange realm where silliness flows.

So let's toast to dreams that run wild,
Where laughter's the language of every child.
In this whimsical place, nobody's mild,
In twilight's embrace, imagination's riled.

Hidden Respite

Behind the curtain of a banana peel,
A disco party with fruit as our meal.
Dancing with pickles, I start to reel,
In this jester's realm, where nonsense is real.

A beach ball rolls with a funny sound,
As jellybeans tumble all over the ground.
Clams take selfies, how comically profound,
In this quirky nook, laughter's unbound.

Lime green frogs wearing glasses, oh my,
Debating the meaning of ice cream pie.
With silly antics, they leap and fly,
Making the evening glow and fly high.

So I'll stay here in this whimsical bliss,
Where the laughter rings clear, and I can't miss.
In a world of chuckles, joy's an abyss,
In this hidden spot, it's pure happiness.

Chasing Sunbeams

In a world of pogo sticks, where shadows dance,
Sunbeams wiggle, in a silly trance.
We dart and weave, just like a fish,
Searching for rays, it's a crazy wish.

The clowns are laughing, as we trip and fall,
Wrestling with sunlight, having a ball.
With ice cream cones that melt so fast,
Silly giggles echo, a joyous blast.

Jumping over puddles, like they're bear traps,
We stumble and tumble, with wild mishaps.
Tickling daisies, we run through the grass,
In this sunbeam chase, no time to be crass.

So grab your shades, let's frolic and play,
In a land of bright lights, we'll laugh all day.
Chasing those beams, till the stars appear,
In this goofy chase, nothing to fear.

Chronicles of Quietude

In a library filled with whispers and sighs,
A sneeze from a cat, and the silence flies.
Pillow forts built from stories untold,
As teddy bears watch, their eyes gleam gold.

Tea parties hosted with biscuits on trays,
While the mice in the corner have raucous play.
The dust bunnies dance, a perplexing sight,
In this soft chaos, all feels just right.

Unicorns bowling on clouds made of fluff,
Eating spaghetti, but it's never enough.
Quietude's laughter, a riddle we share,
With a twist of a plot, we float in the air.

So hush, dear friend, and don't spill the beans,
In this realm of rest, we chase silly dreams.
Each giggle and snort, a sweet serenade,
In the chronicles of quiet, our happiness laid.

Sands of Time

Tick-tock goes the clock, but the sand's in a rush,
Wearing flip-flops, we gather in a hush.
The seconds roll by like a tumbleweed,
As we chase after them, laughter's our creed.

We build castles of whispers, with moats full of fun,
While crabs in tuxedos dance under the sun.
Time's got a wacky, unpredictable flair,
But we wave our hands, surrender and share.

Each grain tells a story, peculiar and bright,
Of pirates and mermaids who giggle at night.
With spoons made of laughter and cups filled with cheer,
We sip from the goblet of nonsense, my dear.

So come take a ride on this clock's silly glide,
In the sands of our jokes, we'll forever abide.
Laughing at time, as it giggles along,
In this playful embrace, where we always belong.

The Quiet Symphony

A symphony of whispers, quiet yet loud,
With frogs playing banjos, we jive with the crowd.
A snail in a top hat leads the grand show,
As crickets tap dance, putting on a glow.

Up high in the trees, the owls play the flute,
While raccoons with cymbals kick up their own loot.
The shy little shadows join in with a shuffle,
Creating a melody that mixes with chuckles.

The moon beams in, wearing shades of surprise,
As stars start to twinkle their sparkly ties.
Each note filled with mischief, every pause a delight,
In this peaceful ruckus, our hearts take flight.

So close your eyes tight, let imaginations steer,
In the quiet of chaos, laughter draws near.
The symphony swells, with giggles galore,
In this realm of stillness, who could ask for more?

Echoes from the Abyss

In the land where the cacti dance,
A lizard dreams of a fleeting chance.
He tries to rain down a cool surprise,
But all he gets is some puzzled flies.

Beneath the sun, the tumbleweeds spin,
A scorpion's grin reveals his kin.
With each little leap, they jump and frolic,
While the stuffy cactus stays quite melancholic.

In this wild mirage, no worries exist,
A chubby coyote writes a cool twist.
He draws up plans to build a home,
But all he finds is a pesky gnome.

So when you wander in search of fun,
Know that mirth dances under the sun.
Take a leap with the lizard and coyote crew,
And join the antics that no one knew!

Untouched Horizons

Out where the clouds wear silly hats,
The gentle breeze flirts with all the bats.
A jolly sunbeam starts a race,
With shadows playing tag in the space.

A unicorn munching on cotton candy,
Claims that the sky is far too randy!
With giggles echoing, it prances light,
While asteroids rave with sheer delight.

Each tumble of earth, each twist and bend,
Builds a haven that's fun to send.
A clam shell whispers to a jellyfish,
"Make a wish, delightful and swish!"

So roll in the grass, let laughter ignite,
With horizons untouched, pure and bright.
Dare to dream, let the world be strange,
Just like that unicorn dancing in range!

Coves of the Heart

In a bay where the starfish try to sing,
They make a band with a golden ring.
Clams tap out a jazzy beat,
While jellyfish dance to the skip of their feet.

A parrot squawks with a wacky grin,
Telling fish tales about where he's been.
Puffer-fish puff, making everyone laugh,
While an octopus juggles a treasure map.

Seashells gossip, spreading the word,
About the dolphin that boldly stirred.
He races waves and chases jellybeans,
Dreaming of life under candy machines.

So come join us, feel the fine art,
In these whimsical coves of the heart.
Where nautical nonsense meets sailor's cheer,
And laughter abounds for all to hear!

Between Fathoms of Thought

In this realm of bubbles and wiggly things,
A goldfish dons an array of rings.
He spins in circles, a shimmering sight,
Chasing a dream that feels just right.

An octopus winks with eight little eyes,
Teaching the crabs to improvise.
With a flip and a flop, they dance on the sand,
Creating a festivity that's truly grand.

They giggle and chortle, nobody's shy,
As seahorses whisper and dolphins fly.
"Why is the sea so deep?" asks a ray,
"We're just trying to jive, come what may!"

So delve into thoughts, don't hold back,
In this underwater world, they keep on track.
Between each fathom and whimsical swirl,
Find the fun and let laughter unfurl!

Solace at Dusk

In a land where sunbeams play,
A cactus wears a hat today.
It tells jokes to a passing breeze,
Tickling the clouds and making them sneeze.

The rabbits dance, they twist and twirl,
While lizards don their finest burl.
They serve up tea in tiny cups,
With crumpets made from sprouted ups.

A hammock swings from tree to tree,
While squirrels chatter merrily.
They toss the nuts and laugh aloud,
Inviting even the tiniest crowd.

As shadows stretch, the fun begins,
With card games led by fox and twins.
The moon peeks through with a wink and grin,
An evening of laughter shall now begin.

Celestial Sanctuary

Stars tumble down like candy bars,
While comets sing in distant guitars.
The moon likes to strut with flair so bright,
Hosting a gala in the velvet night.

The aliens join with their glow-in-the-dark,
Making balloon animals in the park.
They giggle and wiggle in cosmic shorts,
Throwing a bash with intergalactic sports.

Some planets roll dice, while others bake,
With stardust cookies, oh what a shake!
Martians juggling whilst Venus spins,
Each moment filled with whimsical grins.

As the night dips low, they raise a toast,
To dreams swirling like jelly, they love the most.
With sparkles and laughter, they float on by,
In this sanctuary where giggles fly.

Fountain of Serenity

Water splashes with a playful glee,
As frogs wear crowns and sip their tea.
The goldfish teach the otters to dance,
In this fountain, all take a chance.

Butterflies wear shades, looking quite cool,
While dragonflies spin like they're in school.
The turtles crack jokes—oh, what a scene!
In the bubble pops, they're all evergreen.

With ripples and giggles, the spa is grand,
Hosting a splashy, froggy band.
The water's warm, the laughter flows,
As everyone poses with silly toes.

With a flick of the fin, a cannonball dive,
The best of times, where spirits thrive.
The fountain bubbles, life sings along,
In this watery world, we all belong.

Whispers of a Serene Mirage

In a land where puffballs float on air,
The sun wears shades with the utmost care.
A mirage chuckles, casting its spell,
While sandcastles gossip, oh can't you tell?

Camels in shades strut like they own,
While palm trees sway, a dance sweetly known.
They sing serenades to lizards on rocks,
Who dance to the rhythm of tickling socks.

The mirage pranks with a flickering light,
As shadows play tag into the night.
With a burst of laughter, they twirl around,
This whimsical world keeps joy unbound.

In this joyful land, laughter's the guide,
No worries here, just fun and pride.
With whispers of joy and delight so loud,
In this serene mirage, we are all proud.

Silken Sands of Serendipity

In a land where camels wear bright hats,
The sun plays tricks on playful brats.
Turtles race on a beach ball spree,
While seagulls shout, "You can't catch me!"

Jellyfish juggle with jelly beans,
And sandcastles boast of royal scenes.
A parrot sips a piña colada,
Claiming it's the best holiday product.

Laughter rolls like a gentle wave,
Each grain of sand has a joke to save.
Under palm trees, coconuts fall,
Yelling, "Watch out! We're here to brawl!"

Cactus plants try to dance to a tune,
While the moon chuckles, making a swoon.
As night settles with stars so bright,
It whispers, "You won't sleep tonight!"

A Haven of Ethereal Thoughts

In clouds where thoughts float like cotton candy,
An idea hiccups, 'Is that really dandy?'
Mind squirrels team up for a brainstorming jam,
Each nugget of wisdom prefers a glam.

A daydream lounges in a designer chair,
Wearing shades, sipping lemonade without a care.
Ideas shoot like fireflies in a jar,
While giggles invent thoughts from afar.

Minds drift like boats on a marshmallow sea,
Chasing concepts that shout, "Look at me!"
Laughter echoes in the space up high,
Where wishes and chuckles all multiply.

In this haven where whims frolic free,
Even serious thoughts wear a comical spree.
A rainbow thinks it's funny and bright,
As whispers giggle, "Let's party tonight!"

Reflections in a Still Pool

A pond that giggles with rippling tunes,
Frogs sport sunglasses, flirting with moons.
The fish throw parties as crickets knock,
Each splash and croak creates quite a shock.

A snail slides by with a gleaming grin,
Saying, "Bet I'll win if we race for the win!"
Dragonflies wear ties and dance in the light,
While lily pads host a grand disco night.

The reeds sway gently, singing a song,
Of tales where silly hiccups belong.
Mirrors reflect each whimsical sight,
And laughter erupts as bugs take flight.

In this pool where giggles run deep,
Even turtles sigh, "We need more sleep!"
Yet, they stay up for the silly moon's gaze,
Making mischief in endless playful ways.

Echoes of Solitude and Surrender

In the quiet, a echo hums a tune,
As a lone cactus salutes the moon.
A turtle whispers, 'Is anybody out?'
While shadows giggle and weave about.

The wind teases leaves with a silly dance,
As it twirls around, giving dreams a chance.
Alone feels like a game of hide and seek,
Where solitude wears a funny little peak.

A rock sighs deeply, with stories untold,
But with each chuckle, its heart turns bold.
Even the stars roll their eyes in surprise,
At the nonsense brewing beneath distant skies.

In silence, where laughter's deeply nestled,
A wanderer wonders if the world wrestles.
Yet, here in the quiet, joy sings along,
In the echoes of solitude, life hums a song.

Deserted Reverie

In the sand where shadows play,
Lizards dance a jazzy sway.
Cacti wear their prickly hats,
While camels chat with curious cats.

A mirage waves with a cheeky grin,
"Join the fun, let's all jump in!"
But as you leap, oh what a fall,
Turns out it's just a beach ball!

With every tumble, giggles grow,
As tumbleweeds put on a show.
The sun shines bright, not one gray cloud,
We're the silliest troupe in this vast crowd!

In this land, nonsense can thrive,
With rubber ducks that talk and jive.
So grab your snacks and pack your cheer,
In this wacky place, there's nothing to fear!

Hushed Waters

A pond with ducks who sip their tea,
Whispers secrets, just you and me.
Goldfish gossip, "Did you see?
Two frogs croaked opera – what a spree!"

The water's still, yet ripples laugh,
As frogs in tuxedos take a bath.
One makes waves, with a perfect splash,
"Just practicing for my big frog bash!"

Dragonflies wear tiny shades,
While turtles play charades in parades.
A lily pad holds court today,
With all the critters who wish to play.

"Come join us, friend, don't be shy!
We've got snacks – oh my, oh my!"
As laughter melds with sunlit beams,
This tranquil place is full of dreams!

A Mirage Called Tomorrow

A bouncing cloud with jellybeans,
Waves hello to all the scenes.
Tomorrow's here, with sprightly cheer,
Bringing gifts, oh dear, oh dear!

Popcorn trees that crackle pop,
Dancing shadows never stop.
A rain of sprinkles from the sky,
Leaves everyone wondering why.

Silly thoughts take center stage,
As time unwinds, we disengage.
Chronicles of whimsy unfold,
In a land where dreams are bold.

So here we twirl, while giggles fly,
Let's chase the clouds, just you and I.
Tomorrow beckons with glee and cheer,
In this funny place, we disappear!

Sunkissed Reverie

On a beach where chortles ring,
Seagulls practice their opera swing.
Sandcastles with windows bright,
Cheerful crabs join in the light.

Flip-flops fly, a dizzy dance,
As sunbathers give the skies a glance.
"Who threw that?" a little voice cries,
While beach balls soar to sunny highs.

Snorkeling squirrel looks for pearls,
While umbrella drinks swirl and twirl.
The sun waves back with a wink,
"Let's all stretch and give a blink!"

In this space where laughter's free,
Waves conspire in harmony.
So join the fun, don't hesitate,
For in this mirth, we celebrate!

Whispers in the Dunes

Sandy socks and flip-flops too,
Where camels dance and donkeys boo.
A mirage sings a silly tune,
And lights up dreams beneath the moon.

We sip on drinks that taste like sand,
Wishing we could find a band.
With laughter echoing in the breeze,
It's hard to take any of this with ease.

A cactus wearing shades so bright,
He tells us jokes that feel just right.
We roll around and lose all grace,
As grains of sand cover our face.

The stars reply with twinkling eyes,
As tumbleweeds take us by surprise.
In this land where giggles roam,
We've found a place that feels like home.

Mirage of the Heart

A distant castle made of cream,
Where butterflies join in the dream.
We chase our thoughts on sassy kites,
Underneath the sun that brightly bites.

Hiccups from the soda pop,
Bubblegum clouds that never stop.
A jester walks with squeaky shoes,
Offering us some funky views.

He says the pastry's laced with joy,
And every ice cream's just a toy.
With every scoop, it's hearts we mend,
In sticky messes, we find a friend.

We blend our sorrows with sweet glee,
Whispers of laughter, wild and free.
In swirling tales of strange delight,
We dance until the morning light.

Ephemeral Shores

Footprints vanish with each wave,
As seagulls strut, oh so brave.
A treasure chest that's filled with fries,
We feast and giggle at our prize.

Sandcastles rise and tumble down,
While crabs perform their little frown.
We wear our sunglasses upside down,
And laugh till we start to drown.

With beach balls bouncing everywhere,
And sunscreen goo upon our hair.
Each splash, a storyline unfolds,
As we create our world of golds.

Oh, how the tides come in to play,
Chasing our troubles far away.
In this fleeting moment, we're alive,
With silly dreams that help us thrive.

Lullabies of the Night

Starry skies, a winking moon,
A hippo plays a jazzy tune.
Fireflies dance in silly pairs,
While owls wear hats and silly stares.

The camels snore in rhythmic beat,
A choir of frogs tap their feet.
We gather 'round the crackling fire,
Trading jokes that lift us higher.

Ticklish breezes brush our cheeks,
As magic dust flows through our peaks.
With yawns and giggles, dreams take flight,
In this whimsical, starry night.

So close your eyes and join the fun,
Let laughter linger as we run.
In the land where shadows gleam,
We'll stay awake inside a dream.

Dunes of Reverie and Desire

In the sandy hills, I found my shoe,
A lonely cactus wearing my left, too.
Camels play poker, chips made of sand,
Laughing so hard, they can't make a stand.

Napping under palms, I start to doze,
When a sand crab steals my treat—what a pose!
Chasing my snacks, I trip and I roll,
Behold the great tumble, a comedy goal!

Mirages appear, dancing with glee,
A fountain of soda? Is that just for me?
I dive right in, but it's just my luck,
A wave of fizz! Oh, what a muck!

At twilight's hour, we sing silly songs,
With wise old owls who hoot out the wrongs.
In these silly dunes, life's a wild dream,
Where everyone giggles and laughs as a team.

Sanctuary Beneath the Stars

Under the blanket of twinkling lights,
We dance with the shadows, enjoying our nights.
A snail named Gary moves at a crawl,
While I join in grace, tripping over my shawl.

Sipping on punches that sparkle and glow,
I splashed more than drank—what a comedic show!
The moon's my buddy, it winks as I slip,
With each silly moment, we giggle and flip.

A disco ball cactus spins overhead,
Throwing wild patterns—imagine my spread!
The stars give a chorus, a whimsical tune,
Under this sanctuary, I'll dance with the moon!

As I tumble and roll, dust sticks to my face,
"Don't worry!" I chuckle, "It's a stylish embrace!"
In this starry realm, joy cleverly blooms,
Together we laugh, beneath bright cosmic fumes.

Mirage of Hope in the Desert Night

In a shimmering haze, I spot a delight,
A buffet of laughs on this fine desert night.
But wait! It's a mirage—just cookies and cake,
And the dessert's a trick, what a bellyache!

A lizard in sunglasses, so cool on his rock,
Offers me chips from his pocket-sized stock.
His buddies all gather, they start a new game,
Playing leapfrog with dreams, oh what a wild claim!

A giant's shadow looms, but don't be afraid,
He's just here for snacks, like a fragrant parade.
Together we giggle at our little plight,
In the mischief of mirages we find pure delight!

When dawn creeps in, it's a relishing sight,
We put on our shades, feeling just so bright.
In this nightly dance, our laughter was spun,
Even the sun joins, and says, "Let's have fun!"

Where Imagination Blooms

In a garden of thoughts, where daydreams take flight,
I found my lost marbles, still glowing so bright.
A dandelion king spins tales of grand quests,
While giggling fairies host their whimsical fests.

Clouds wear hats that they've borrowed from sheep,
As I slide down rainbows, laughing in heaps.
The ground's made of marshmallows, a squishy delight,
Bouncing and hoping, through day into night.

A chipmunk with glasses gives sage advice,
"Life is just better with sprinkles and rice!"
Treats raining down, what a glorious bloom,
Together we dance in this sugary room!

As twilight sets in, only giggles remain,
In this world of wonders, we've tossed aside pain.
Imagination blooms, like flowers in light,
In laughter and joy, we take our great flight.

www.ingramcontent.com/pod-product-compliance
Lightning Source LLC
Chambersburg PA
CBHW072213070526
44585CB00015B/1323